HIS INSPIRED WORD,

My INSPIRED Thoughts

HIS INSPIRED WORD, My INSPIRED Thoughts

by
Ellouise Cochrane

PUBLISHING
Christian Literature & Artwork
A BOLD TRUTH Publication

HIS INSPIRED WORD, My INSPIRED Thoughts
Copyright © 2015 Ellouise Cochrane

ISBN 13: 978-0-9972586-1-5

BOLD TRUTH PUBLISHING
Christian Literature & Artwork
300 West 41st
Sand Springs, Oklahoma 74063
www.BoldTruthPublishing.com
beirep@yahoo.com

Printed in the USA.

We would like to recognize and thank these Publiishers, for publishing and distributing the following versions of God's written Word.

The Lord gave the word: great was the company of those that published it. - Psalm 68:11 (KJV)

Contents

HIS INSPIRED WORD
In Alphabetical Order

Dedication

This book is dedicated first and foremost to my Daddy, God, because He formed within me creative abilities for the use of furthering His Kingdom. What a privilege to provide God's Word to others as they travel along their personal journey of getting to know Him through knowing His Word. I am forever grateful to Him for giving me the wisdom to pen these words on paper.

I also want to dedicate this book to my Mother, Minola, and my Father, Clarence. For years I didn't understand the magnitude of blessing that you bestowed upon me as your Daughter. Over the past few years I began seeking out the What and the Why for being born because I desired to know my true purpose. As a result I discovered wonderful revelations about my inheritance which has connected me to my path of destiny.

I am WHO I am because of you. This book would not be possible without ALL of your (God, Mom & Dad's) loving investments in my life, and the rich deposits you contribute(d). I will always love YOU!!!

Thank you for your continued support from the Throne Room and the Cloud of Witnesses!

Introduction

Hello Dear Friends,

THANK YOU! Thank you for believing in me and buying my book.

Please accept my personal invitation to join me for daily inspiration and growth through studying God's Word. I pray you will carefully explore this Devotional and truly get to know God more deeply through knowing His Word. It is my privilege to provide you with this special opportunity to experience a unique transformation as a result of the daily nourishing of your soul. I hope that you will challenge yourself to meditate only on thoughts that are admirable, pure, true, lovely, good, and honorable.

Life experiences are as unique as each individual, so please feel free to begin your 'week' on which ever day suits you best. Give yourself permission to enjoy meditating on these Scriptures selected for building blocks to empowerment, and become inspired to the point that your thought processes overflow onto the page, leading to the creation of your own weekly journal & devotional.

Remember you cannot finish what you do not start...

...READY, SET, GO!

His Word

● First Word

CREATED ~ So God **created** man in His own image; in the image of God He created him; male and female He created them. *(Gen. 1 27 NKJV)*

● Second Word

GOD ~ Now to the King eternal, immortal, invisible, the only **God**, be honor and glory forever and ever. Amen. *(1 Tim. 1:17 NIV)*

● Third Word

EVERLASTING ~ Do you not know? Have you not heard? The LORD is the **everlasting** God, the Creator of the ends of the earth. He will not grow tired or weary, and his understanding no one can fathom. *(Isaiah 40:28 NIV)*

My Thoughts

His Word

• First Word

EQUIP ~ 11 So Christ himself gave the apostles, the prophets, the evangelists, the pastors and teachers, 12 to **equip** his people for works of service, so that the body of Christ may be built up.
(Eph. 4:11-12 NIV)

• Second Word

TOGETHER ~ My goal is that their hearts, having been knit **together** in love, may be encouraged, and that they may have all the riches that assurance brings in their understanding of the knowledge of the mystery of God, namely, Christ. *(Col. 2:2 NET)*

• Third Word

UNITY ~ Until we all reach **unity** in the faith and in the knowledge of the Son of God and become mature, attaining to the whole measure of the fullness of Christ. *(Eph. 4:13 NIV)*

My Thoughts

_____

_____

_____

_____

_____

_____

_____

_____

_____

_____

_____

_____

_____

_____

_____

_____

_____

_____

_____

His Word

• First Word

CONFIDENT ~ For I am **confident** of this very thing, that He who began a good work in you will perfect it until the day of Christ Jesus. *(Phil. 1:6 NASB)*

• Second Word

FAITHFULNESS ~ It is of the LORD's mercies that we are not consumed, because his compassions fail not. They are new every morning: great is thy **faithfulness**. *(Lam 3:22-23 KJV)*

• Third Word

PROMISES ~ By which have been given to us exceedingly great and precious **promises**, that through these you may be partakers of the divine nature. *(2 Peter 1:4 NKJV)*

My Thoughts

His Word

● First Word

ABUNDANTLY ~ The thief does not come except to steal, and to kill, and to destroy. I have come that they may have life, and that they may have it more **abundantly.** *(John 10:10 NKJV)*

● Second Word

BLESSED ~ All praise to God, the Father of our Lord Jesus Christ, who has **blessed** us with every spiritual blessing in the heavenly realms because we are united with Christ. *(Eph. 1:3 NLT)*

● Third Word

RICHES ~ And my God will supply all your needs according to His **riches i**n glory in Christ Jesus. *(Phil. 4:19 NASB)*

My Thoughts

His Word

● First Word

ENEMIES ~ When a person's ways are pleasing to the LORD, he makes even his **enemies** to be at peace with him. *(Prov. 16:7 GW)*

● Second Word

OVERCOME ~ You are of God, little children, and have **overcome** them because greater is he that is in you, than he that is in the world.
(1 John 4:4 NKJV)

● Third Word

PEACE ~ **Peace** I leave with you, My **peace** I give to you; not as the world gives do I give to you. Let not your heart be troubled, neither let it be afraid.
(John 14:27 NKJV)

My Thoughts

His Word

• First Word

DECREE ~ I issue a **decree** that in every part of my kingdom people must fear and reverence the God of Daniel. For he is the living God and he endures forever; his kingdom will not be destroyed, his dominion will never end. *(Dan. 6:26 NIV)*

• Second Word

ESTABLISH ~ And let the beauty of the LORD our God be upon us, and **establish** the work of our hands for us; yes, **establish** the work of our hands. *(Psalm 90:17 NKJV)*

• Third Word

FULFILLED ~ And He began to say to them, "Today this Scripture has been **fulfilled** in your hearing. *(Luke 4:21 NASB)*

12

My Thoughts

His Word

• First Word

DISCOVER ~ Examine me, O God, and know my mind; test me, and **discover** my thoughts.
(Psalm 139:23 GNT)

• Second Word

SEEK ~ But **seek** first the kingdom of God and His righteousness, and all these things shall be added to you. *(Matt. 6:33 NKJV)*

• Third Word

PRESENCE ~ You will show me the path of life; In Your **presence** is fullness of joy; At your right hand are pleasures forevermore. *(Psalm 16:11 NKJV)*

My Thoughts

_____

_____

_____

_____

_____

_____

_____

_____

_____

_____

_____

_____

_____

_____

_____

_____

_____

_____

_____

_____

_____

_____

His Word

• First Word

AGAINST ~ What then shall we say to these things? If God is for us, who can be **against** us.
(Rom. 8:31 KJV)

• Second Word

NEED ~ And my God shall supply all your **need** according to His riches in glory by Christ Jesus.
(Phil. 4:19 NKJV)

• Third Word

VICTORY ~ But thanks be to God, who gives us the **victory** through our Lord Jesus Christ.
(1 Cor. 15:57 NKJV)

My Thoughts

His Word

● First Word

HEALED ~ He said to her, Daughter, your faith has **healed** you. Go in peace and be freed from your suffering. *(Mark 5:34 NIV)*

● Second Word

MERRY ~ A **merry** heart does good, like medicine, but a broken spirit dries the bones. *(Prov. 17:22 NKJV)*

● Third Word

SATISFY ~ I will **satisfy** you with a long life. I will show you how I will save you. *(Psalm 91:16 GW)*

My Thoughts

His Word

• First Word

FOREVER ~ For the LORD is good and his love endures **forever**; his faithfulness continues through all generations. *(Psalm 100:5 NIV)*

• Second Word

GOODNESS ~ Or do you despise the riches of His **goodness**, forbearance, and longsuffering, not knowing that the **goodness** of God leads you to repentance. *(Rom. 2:4 NKJV)*

• Third Word

TASTE ~ Oh, **taste** and see that the LORD is good; Blessed is the man who trusts in Him. *(Psalm 34:8 NKJV)*

My Thoughts

_____

_____

_____

_____

_____

_____

_____

_____

_____

_____

_____

_____

_____

_____

_____

_____

_____

_____

_____

_____

_____

His Word

• First Word

GROW ~ But **grow** in the grace and knowledge of our Lord and Savior Jesus Christ. To Him be the glory, both now and to the day of eternity. Amen. *(2 Pet. 3:18 NASB)*

• Second Word

KNOWLEDGE ~ The fear of the Lord is the beginning of **knowledge**; Fools despise wisdom and instruction. *(Prov. 1:7 NASB)*

• Third Word

WISDOM ~ If any of you lacks **wisdom**, you should ask God, who gives generously to all without finding fault, and it will be given to you. *(James 1:5 NIV)*

My Thoughts

His Word

● First Word

COMMITTED ~ Train me in good common sense; I'm thoroughly **committed** to living your way.
(Psalm 119:66 MSG)

● Second Word

HEART ~ I will give you a new **heart** and put a new spirit within you; I will take the **heart** of stone out of your flesh and give you a **heart** of flesh.
(Ezekiel 36:26 NKJV)

● Third Word

RIGHTEOUSNESS ~ Little children, make sure no one deceives you; the one who practices **righteousness** is righteous, just as He is righteous.
(1 John 3:7 NASB)

My Thoughts

His Word

● First Word

ATTENTION ~ Till I come, give **attention** to reading, to exhortation, to doctrine.
(1 Tim. 4:13 NKJV)

● Second Word

LISTEN ~ He said, "If you will **listen** carefully to the LORD your God and do what he considers right, if you pay attention to his commands and obey all his laws, I will never make you suffer any of the diseases I made the Egyptians suffer, because I am the LORD, who heals you." *(Exodus 15:26 NKJV)*

● Third Word

WORD ~ Your **word** is a lamp to my feet and a light to my path. *(Psalm 119:105 NASB)*

My Thoughts

His Word

● First Word

JOY ~ Nehemiah said, "Go and enjoy choice food and sweet drinks, and send some to those who have nothing prepared. This day is holy to our Lord. Do not grieve, for the **joy** of the LORD is your strength. *(Nehemiah 8:10 NIV)*

● Second Word

POWER ~ Behold, I have given you authority to tread on serpents and scorpions, and over all the **power** of the enemy, and nothing will injure you. *(Luke 10:19 NASB)*

● Third Word

STRENGTH ~ But those who hope in the LORD will renew their **strength**. *(Isaiah 40:31 NIV)*

My Thoughts

His Word

● First Word

FAVOR ~ Blessed (happy, fortunate, to be envied) are the people who know the joyful sound [who understand and appreciate the spiritual blessings symbolized by the feasts]; they walk, O Lord, in the light and **favor** of Your countenance. *(Psalm 89:15 AMP)*

● Second Word

GIFT ~ For the wages of sin is death, but the free **gift** of God is eternal life in Christ Jesus our Lord. *(Rom. 6:23 NASB)*

● Third Word

HEALING ~ But to you who fear My name The Sun of Righteousness shall arise With **healing** in His wings; And you shall go out and grow fat like stall-fed calves. *(Malachi 4:2 NKJV)*

My Thoughts

_____

_____

_____

_____

_____

_____

_____

_____

_____

_____

_____

_____

_____

_____

_____

_____

_____

_____

_____

_____

His Word

• First Word

JUSTICE ~ How blessed are those who keep **justice**, who practice righteousness at all times.
(Psalm 106:3 NASB)

• Second Word

RIGHTEOUS ~ The fear of the LORD is clean, enduring forever; The judgments of the LORD are true; they are **righteous** altogether.
(Psalm 19:9 NASB)

• Third Word

UPRIGHT ~ Be glad in the Lord and rejoice, you righteous ones; And shout for joy, all you who are **upright** in heart. *(Psalm 32:11 NASB)*

My Thoughts

His Word

● First Word

ETERNAL LIFE ~ For the wages of sin is death, but the gift of God is **eternal life** in Christ Jesus our Lord. *(Rom. 6:23 NIV)*

● Second Word

REWARD ~ 23 Whatever you do, work at it with all your heart, as working for the Lord, not for human masters,
24 since you know that you will receive an inheritance from the Lord as a **reward**. It is the Lord Christ you are serving. *(Col. 3:23-24 NIV)*

● Third Word

SALVATION ~ For He says in an acceptable time I have heard you, and in the day of **salvation** I have helped you. Behold, now is the accepted time; behold, now is the day of **salvation.**
(2 Cor. 6:2 NKJV)

My Thoughts

His Word

● First Word

LAUGHING ~ He will yet fill your mouth with **laughing**, and your lips with rejoicing. *(Job 8:21 NKJV)*

● Second Word

REJOICE ~ Be glad, people of Zion, **rejoice** in the LORD your God, for he has given you the autumn rains because he is faithful. He sends you abundant showers, both autumn and spring rains, as before. *(Joel 2:23 NIV)*

● Third Word

SHOUT ~ Sing for joy to God our strength; **shout** aloud to the God of Jacob. *(Psalm 81:1 NIV)*

My Thoughts

_____

_____

_____

_____

_____

_____

_____

_____

_____

_____

_____

_____

_____

_____

_____

_____

_____

_____

_____

_____

_____

_____

_____

His Word

• First Word

COUNSEL ~ Blessed is the man Who walks not in the **counsel** of the ungodly, nor stands in the path of sinners, nor sits in the seat of the scornful.
(Psalm 1:1 NKJV)

• Second Word

FREE ~ Therefore if the Son makes you **free**, you shall be **free** indeed. *(John 8:36 NKJV)*

• Third Word

PROPHECY ~ Knowing this first, that no **prophecy** of scripture is of private interpretation.
(2 Peter 1:20 ASV)

My Thoughts

_____

_____

_____

_____

_____

_____

_____

_____

_____

_____

_____

_____

_____

_____

_____

_____

_____

_____

_____

_____

_____

His Word

Week 20

• First Word

CHRIST ~ Simon Peter answered and said, "You are the **Christ**, the Son of the living God.
(Matt 16:16 NKJV)

• Second Word

LAMB ~ Saying with a loud voice, worthy is the **lamb** that was slain to receive power, and riches, and wisdom, and strength, and honor, and glory, and blessing *(Rev. 5:12 KJV)*

• Third Word

LION ~ But one of the elders said to me, "Do not weep. Behold, the **Lion** of the tribe of Judah, the Root of David, has prevailed to open the scroll and to loose its seven seals. *(Rev 5:5 NKJV)*

My Thoughts

His Word

• First Word

HOLY SPIRIT ~ But you shall receive power when the **Holy Spirit** has come upon you; and you shall be witnesses to Me in Jerusalem, and in all Judea and Samaria, and to the end of the earth. *(Acts 1:8 NKJV)*

• Second Word

LIGHT ~ When Jesus spoke again to the people, he said, "I am the **light** of the world. Whoever follows me will never walk in darkness, but will have the **light** of life. *(John 8:12 NIV)*

• Third Word

TRUTH ~ O send out Your light and Your **truth**, let them lead me; let them bring me to Your holy hill and to your dwelling places. *(Psalm 43:3 NASB)*

My Thoughts

His Word

● First Word

FAITH ~ Looking unto Jesus, the author and finisher of our **faith**, who for the joy that was set before Him endured the cross, despising the shame, and has sat down at the right hand of the throne of God.
(Heb. 12:2 NKJV)

● Second Word

HOPE ~ Now may the God of **hope** fill you with all joy and peace in believing, so that you will abound in **hope** by the power of the Holy Spirit.
(Rom 15:13 NASB)

● Third Word

LOVE ~ And he answered, You shall love the Lord your God with all your heart, and with all your soul, and with all your strength, and with all your mind; and your neighbor as yourself.
(Luke 10:27 NASB)

My Thoughts

His Word

• First Word

ABIDE ~ If you **abide** in Me, and My words **abide** in you, you will ask what you desire, and it shall be done for you. *(John 15:7 NKJV)*

• Second Word

INSPIRATION ~ All scripture is given by **inspiration** of God, and is profitable for doctrine, for reproof, for correction, for instruction in righteousness. *(2 Tim. 3:16 KJV)*

• Third Word

PROFIT ~ For indeed we have had good news preached to us, just as they also; but the word they heard did not **profit** them, because it was not united by faith in those who heard. *(Heb. 4:2 NASB)*

My Thoughts

His Word

• First Word

PRAYER ~ Therefore I tell you, whatever you ask for in **prayer**, believe that you have received it, and it will be yours. *(Mark 11:24 NIV)*

• Second Word

SUPPLICATIONS ~ I said to the LORD, "You are my God; Give ear, O LORD, to the voice of my **supplications**. *(Psalm 140:6 NASB)*

• Third Word

THANKSGIVING ~ The LORD will surely comfort Zion and will look with compassion on all her ruins; he will make her deserts like Eden, her wastelands like the garden of the LORD. Joy and gladness will be found in her, **thanksgiving** and the sound of singing. *(Isaiah 51:3 NIV)*

My Thoughts

His Word

● First Word

AUTHORITY ~ Then the end will come, when he hands over the kingdom to God the Father after he has destroyed all dominion, **authority** and power. *(1 Cor. 15:24 NASB)*

● Second Word

KING ~ And He has on His robe and on His thigh a name written **King** of Kings and Lord of Lords. *(Rev. 19:16 NKJV)*

● Third Word

ROCK ~ The LORD is my **rock**, my fortress and my deliverer; my God is my **rock**, in whom I take refuge, my shield and the horn of my salvation, my stronghold. *(Psalm 18:2 NIV)*

My Thoughts

His Word

• First Word

MEDITATE ~ This Book of the Law shall not depart from your mouth, but you shall **meditate** in it day and night, that you may observe to do according to all that is written in it. For then you will make your way prosperous, and then you will have good success. *(Joshua 1:8 NJKV)*

• Second Word

PRAY ~ Therefore confess your sins to each other and **pray** for each other so that you may be healed. The prayer of a righteous person is powerful and effective. *(Jas. 5:16 NIV)*

• Third Word

TRUE ~ Finally, brethren, whatever is **true**, whatever is honorable, whatever is right, whatever is pure, whatever is lovely, whatever is of good repute, if there is any excellence and if anything worthy of praise, dwell on these things. *(Phil. 4:8 NASB)*

My Thoughts

His Word

● First Word

NEAR ~ The Lord is **near** to all who call upon Him, to all who call upon Him in truth.
(Psalm 145:18 NASB)

● Second Word

PATIENCE ~ May the Lord bring you into an ever deeper understanding of the love of God and of the **patience** that comes from Christ.
(2 Thess. 3:5 TLB)

● Third Word

UNDERSTANDING ~ Trust in the LORD with all your heart and do not lean on your own **understanding.** *(Prov. 3:5 NASB)*

My Thoughts

His Word

● First Word

DISCIPLES ~ Therefore go and make **disciples** of all nations, baptizing them in the name of the Father and of the Son and of the Holy Spirit.
(Matt. 28:19 NIV)

● Second Word

PRIEST ~ And he says in another place, you are a **priest** forever, in the order of Melchizedek
(Heb. 5:6 NIV)

● Third Word

MERCIES ~ I beseech you therefore, brethren, by the **mercies** of God, that ye present your bodies a living sacrifice, holy, acceptable unto God, which is your reasonable service. *(Rom. 12:1 KJV)*

My Thoughts

His Word

• First Word

GENERATIONS ~ But I show mercy to thousands of **generations** of those who love me and obey my commandments. *(Exod. 20:6 GW)*

• Second Word

NATIONS ~ From one man he made all the **nations**, that they should inhabit the whole earth; and he marked out their appointed times in history and the boundaries of their lands. *(Acts 17:26 NIV)*

• Third Word

REFUGE ~ O Lord, you have been our **refuge** throughout every generation. *(Psalm 90:1 GW)*

My Thoughts

His Word

● First Word

COURAGEOUS ~ Be strong and very **courageous**. Be careful to obey all the law my servant Moses gave you; do not turn from it to the right or to the left, that you may be successful wherever you go. *(Joshua 1:7 NIV)*

● Second Word

HUMILITY ~ Seek the LORD, all you humble of the land, you who do what he commands. Seek righteousness, seek **humility**. *(Zephaniah 2:3 NASB)*

● Third Word

INTEGRITY ~ Let **integrity** and uprightness preserve me, For I wait for You. *(Psalm 25:21 NKJV)*

My Thoughts

His Word

● First Word

COVENANT ~ 3 You said, I have made a **covenant** with my chosen one, I have sworn to David my servant, 4 I will establish your line forever and make your throne firm through all generations.
(Psalm 89:3-4 NIV)

● Second Word

PROSPER ~ Beloved, I pray above all things that you may **prosper** and be in health, even as your soul **prospers**. *(3 John 1:2 NKJV)*

● Third Word

WEALTH ~ And you shall remember the LORD your God, for it is He who gives you power to get **wealth**, that He may establish His covenant which He swore to your fathers, as it is this day. *(Deut. 8:18 NKJV)*

My Thoughts

His Word

• First Word

BELIEVE ~ So they said **believe** on the Lord Jesus Christ, and you will be saved, you and your household. *(Acts 16:31 NKJV)*

• Second Word

ETERNITY ~ He has made everything beautiful in its time. Also He has put **eternity** in their hearts, except that no one can find out the work that God does from beginning to end. *(Ecclesiastes 3:11 NKJV)*

• Third Word

OBEDIENCE ~ casting down arguments and every high thing that exalts itself against the knowledge of God, bringing every thought into captivity to the **obedience** of Christ. *(2 Cor. 10:5 NKJV)*

My Thoughts

His Word

• First Word

DECLARE ~ Moreover, brethren, I **declare** to you the gospel which I preached to you, which also you received and in which you stand. *(1 Cor. 15:1 NKJV)*

• Second Word

FAITHFUL ~ If we confess our sins, He is **faithful** and just to forgive us our sins and to cleanse us from all unrighteousness. *(1 John 1:9 NKJV)*

• Third Word

TESTIMONY ~ But the **testimony** which I receive is not from man, but I say these things so that you may be saved. *(John 5:34 NASB)*

My Thoughts

His Word   Week 34

● First Word

APOSTLES ~ They were continually devoting themselves to the **apostles'** teaching and to fellowship, to the breaking of bread and to prayer.
(Acts 2:42 NASB)

● Second Word

EVANGELISTS ~ 11 And He Himself gave some to be apostles, some prophets, some **evangelists**, and some pastors and teachers,
12 for the equipping of the saints for the work of ministry, for the edifying of the body of Christ. *(Eph. 4:11-12 NKJV)*

● Third Word

PASTORS ~ And I will give you **pastors** according to mine heart, which shall feed you with knowledge and understanding. *(Jeremiah 3:14 KJV)*

My Thoughts

His Word

• First Word

FRUIT ~ You didn't choose me, but I chose you. I have appointed you to go, to produce **fruit** that will last, and to ask the Father in my name to give you whatever you ask for. *(John 15:16 GW)*

• Second Word

KINDNESS ~ The LORD appeared to us in the past, saying I have loved you with an everlasting love; I have drawn you with unfailing **kindness**.
(Jeremiah 31:3 NIV)

• Third Word

SACRIFICE ~ Through Jesus, therefore, let us continually offer to God a **sacrifice** of praise—the fruit of lips that openly profess his name.
(Heb. 13:15 NIV)

My Thoughts

His Word

● First Word

FATHER ~ So when you pray, you should pray like this: Our **Father** in heaven, may your name always be kept holy [Hallowed be your name].
(Matthew 6:9 EXB)

● Second Word

GODLINESS ~ As His divine power has given to us all things that pertain to life and **godliness**, through the knowledge of Him who called us by glory and virtue. *(2 Peter 1:3 NKJV)*

● Third Word

SHEPHERD ~ The LORD is my **shepherd**, I shall not want. *(Psalm 23:1 NASB)*

My Thoughts

His Word

• First Word

BELIEVERS ~ Don't let anyone look down on you because you are young, but set an example for the **believers** in speech, in conduct, in love, in faith and in purity. *(1 Tim. 4:12 NIV)*

• Second Word

KEEP ~ You will **keep** in perfect peace those whose minds are steadfast, because they trust in you. *(Isaiah 26:3 NIV)*

• Third Word

OBEY ~ So Samuel said has the LORD as great delight in burnt offerings and sacrifices as in **obeying** the voice of the LORD? Behold, to **obey** is better than sacrifice and to heed than the fat of rams. *(1 Sam. 15:22 NKJV)*

My Thoughts

His Word

● First Word

NEW ~ Behold, I will do a **new** thing, Now it shall spring forth; Shall you not know it? I will even make a road in the wilderness and rivers in the desert. *(Isaiah 43:19 GW)*

● Second Word

PROPHETS ~ When the Lord GOD decides to do something, he will first tell his servants, the **prophets.** *(Amos 3:7 ERV)*

● Third Word

VISION ~ And the LORD answered me: write the **vision**; make it plain upon tablets, so he may run who reads it. *(Habakkuk 2:2 RSV)*

My Thoughts

His Word

● First Word

BLESSING ~ The **blessing** of the LORD makes one rich, and He adds no sorrow with it.
(Proverbs 10:22 NKJV)

● Second Word

PROSPERITY ~ Let them shout for joy and be glad, who favor my righteous cause; and let them say continually, "Let the LORD be magnified, who has pleasure in the **prosperity** of His servant.
(Psalm 35:27 NKJV)

● Third Word

LIFE ~ Jesus answered, "I am the way and the truth and the **life**. No one comes to the Father except through me. *(John 14:6 NIV)*

My Thoughts

His Word

● First Word

ABLE ~ And God is **able** to bless you abundantly, so that in all things at all times, having all that you need, you will abound in every good work.
(2 Cor. 9:8 NIV)

● Second Word

GREAT ~ **Great** is the LORD, and most worthy of praise, in the city of our God, his holy mountain.
(Psalm 48:1 NIV)

● Third Word

HOLY ~ Because it is written, "Be **holy**, for I am **holy**.
(1 Peter 1:16 NKJV)

My Thoughts

His Word

• First Word

CHILDREN ~ Behold, **children** are the heritage of the LORD, The fruit of the womb is His reward. *(Psalm 127:3 KJV)*

• Second Word

HEAVEN ~ For our citizenship is in **heaven**, from which also we eagerly wait for a Savior, the Lord Jesus Christ. *(Phil. 3:20 NASB)*

• Third Word

PEOPLE ~ If my **people**, who are called by my name, will humble themselves and pray and seek my face and turn from their wicked ways, then I will hear from heaven, and I will forgive their sin and will heal their land. *(2 Chron. 7:14 NIV)*

My Thoughts

His Word

● First Word

JESUS ~ And she will bring forth a Son, and you shall call His name **JESUS**, for He will save His people from their sins. *(Matthew 1:21 NKJV)*

● Second Word

REDEEMER ~ Thus says the Lord, the King of Israel and his **redeemer**, the Lord of hosts, I am the first and I am the last, and there is no God besides Me. *(Isaiah 44:6 NASB)*

● Third Word

SAVIOR ~ And we have seen and testify that the Father has sent the Son as **Savior** of the world. *(1 John 4:14 NKJV)*

My Thoughts

His Word

● First Word

FREEDOM ~ It is for **freedom** that Christ has set us free. Stand firm, then, and do not let yourselves be burdened again by a yoke of slavery.
(Gal. 5:1 NIV)

● Second Word

LIBERTY ~ Now the Lord is the Spirit; and where the Spirit of the Lord is, there is **liberty**.
(2 Cor. 3:17 NKJV)

● Third Word

MERCY ~ For he said to Moses, I will have **mercy** on whom I have **mercy**, and I will have compassion on whom I have compassion. *(Rom. 8:15 NIV)*

My Thoughts

His Word

• First Word

FORGIVE ~ If my people, who are called by my name, will humble themselves and pray and seek my face and turn from their wicked ways, then I will hear from heaven, and I will **forgive** their sin and will heal their land. *(2 Chron. 7:14 NIV)*

• Second Word

GRACE ~ But he said to me, "My **grace** is sufficient for you, for my power is made perfect in weakness." Therefore I will boast all the more gladly about my weaknesses, so that Christ's power may rest on me. *(2 Cor. 12:9 NIV)*

• Third Word

MERCIFUL ~ Therefore be **merciful**, just as your Father also is **merciful**. *(Luke 6:36 NKJV)*

My Thoughts

His Word

● First Word

PROFITABLE ~ All Scripture is given by inspiration of God, and is **profitable** for doctrine, for reproof, for correction, for instruction in righteousness.
(2 Tim. 3:16 NKJV)

● Second Word

MEDITATION ~ Let the words of my mouth and the **meditation** of my heart be acceptable in Your sight, O LORD, my strength and my redeemer.
(Psalm 19:14 NKJV)

● Third Word

PLANS ~ For I know the **plans** I have for you, declares the LORD, **plans** to prosper you and not to harm you, **plans** to give you hope and a future.
(Jer. 29:11 NIV)

My Thoughts

His Word

● First Word

REDEMPTION ~ But when these things begin to take place, straighten up and lift up your heads, because your **redemption** is drawing near.
(Luke 21:28 NASB)

● Second Word

ANGELS ~ For it is written He shall give His **angels** charge over you, to keep you. *(Luke 4:10 NKJV)*

● Third Word

LIVE ~ I have been crucified with Christ and I no longer **live**, but Christ **lives** in me. The life I now **live** in the body, I **live** by faith in the Son of God, who loved me and gave himself for me. *(Gal. 2:20 NIV)*

My Thoughts

His Word

• First Word

KEYS ~ And I will give you the **keys** of the kingdom of heaven, and whatever you bind on earth will be bound in heaven, and whatever you loose on earth will be loosed in heaven. *(Matthew 16:19 NKJV)*

• Second Word

PROSPEROUS ~ This Book of the Law shall not depart from your mouth, but you shall meditate in it day and night, that you may observe to do according to all that is written in it. For then you will make your way **prosperous**, and then you will have good success. *(Joshua 1:8 NKJV)*

• Third Word

VOLUME ~ Then said I, Lo, I come: in the **volume** of the book it is written of me. *(Psalm 40:7 KJV)*

My Thoughts

His Word

• First Word

OPEN ~ I know your works. See, I have set before you an **open** door, and no one can shut it; for you have a little strength, have kept My word, and have not denied My name. *(Rev. 3:8 NKJV)*

• Second Word

CHILD ~ Train up a **child** in the way he should go, and when he is old he will not depart from it.
(Prov. 22:6 NKJV)

• Third Word

CALLS ~ For "whoever **calls** on the name of the LORD shall be saved. *(Rom. 10:13 NKJV)*

My Thoughts

His Word

● First Word

ANOINTING ~ But you have an **anointing** from the Holy One, and you know all things.
(1 John 2:20 NKJV)

● Second Word

CALLING ~ Who has saved us and called us with a holy **calling**, not according to our works, but according to His own purpose and grace which was given to us in Christ Jesus before time began.
(2 Tim. 1:9 NKJV)

● Third Word

PURPOSE ~ The LORD will fulfill his **purpose** for me; your steadfast love, O LORD, endures forever. Do not forsake the work of your hands.
(Psalm 138:8 ESV)

My Thoughts

_____

_____

_____

_____

_____

_____

_____

_____

_____

_____

_____

_____

_____

_____

_____

_____

_____

_____

_____

_____

_____

His Word

● First Word

GENTLENESS ~ You have also given me the shield of Your salvation; Your right hand has held me up, Your **gentleness** has made me great.
(Psalm 18:35 NKJV)

● Second Word

REMNANT ~ Listen to Me, O house of Jacob, and all the **remnant** of the house of Israel, you who have been borne by Me from birth and have been carried from the womb. *(Isaiah 46:3 NASB)*

● Third Word

WORK ~ And we know that all things **work** together for good for those who love God, who are called according to his purpose. *(Rom. 8:28 NET)*

My Thoughts

His Word

● First Word

BLESS ~ Bless the LORD, O my soul; and all that is within me, **bless** His holy name.
(Psalm 103:1 NKJV)

● Second Word

SING ~ Sing to the LORD a new song; **sing** to the LORD, all the earth. *(Psalm 96:1 NIV)*

● Third Word

WALK ~ I say then **walk** in the Spirit, and you shall not fulfill the lust of the flesh. *(Gal. 5:16 NKJV)*

My Thoughts

His Word

● First Word

LEARN ~ Our people must also **learn** to engage in good deeds to meet pressing needs, so that they will not be unfruitful. *(Titus 3:14 NASB)*

● Second Word

PROPHESY ~ For ye all can **prophesy** one by one, that all may learn, and all may be exhorted. *(1 Cor. 14:31 ASV)*

● Third Word

TEACHERS ~ After all, though you should have ten thousand **teachers** [guides to direct you] in Christ, yet you do not have many fathers. For I became your father in Christ Jesus through the glad tidings [the Gospel]. *(1 Cor. 4:15 AMP)*

My Thoughts

Check out these other Great Books from BOLD TRUTH PUBLISHING

by Adrienne Gottlieb

• ISRAEL'S LEGITIMACY
Why We Should Protect Israel At All Cost

• The Replacement Theology LIE
The Book Jews wished every Christian would read

-----

by Daryl Holloman

• Seemed Good to The Holy Ghost
Inspired Teachings by Brother Daryl
PLUS - Prophecies spoken in Pardo, Cebu, Philippines

• The Adventures of Hezekiah Hare & Ernie Byrd
A Children's Bible Adventure

• Further Adventures
More Good News as Hezekiah & Ernie follow Jesus.

-----

by Steve Young

• SIX FEET DEEP
Burying Your Past with Forgiveness

-----

by Paul Howard

• THE FAITH WALK
Keys to walking in VICTORY!

------

by Joe Waggnor

• Bless THE KING
Praise Poems for My Lord and Saviour

by Jerry W. Hollenbeck
• The KINGDOM of GOD
An Agrarian Society
*Featuring The Kingdom Realities, Bible Study Course,
Research and Development Classes*

• The Word of God
FATHER • WORD • SPIRIT
Literally THE WORD

-----

by Ed Marr
• C. H. P.
Coffee Has Priority
The Memoirs of a California Highway Patrol - Badge 9045

-----

by Elizabeth Pruitt Sloan
• The Holy Spirit SPEAKS Expressly

-----

by James Jonsten
• WHO is GOD to YOU?
The path to know the most misunderstood name in the universe.

-----

by Aaron Jones
• In the SECRET PLACE of THE MOST HIGH
God's Word for Supernatural Healing, Deliverance and Protection

• SOUND from HEAVEN
Praying in Tongues for a Victorious Life

See more Books and all of our products at
www.BoldTruthPublishing.com

THE
EMPOWERED
LIFE SERIES WITH ELLOUISE COCHRANE

CONTACT INFO:
PHONE: 918-852-3170   **E-MAIL:** TRUSTINGELLE@GMAIL.COM

PREREQUISITE(S)
A DESIRE AND WILLINGNESS TO BE TRANSFORMED

In this course you will learn to confront negative thoughts and emotions that cloud proper perspectives for living life at its fullest! Classes offer LIFE - Liberating, Innovative, Fantabulous, Empowerment to embrace struggles , and move past blockages while realizing you possess more than ordinary significance. The confirmed result will be substantial evidence that you love the life you live, which will be apparent for all to see.   After all, as long as you have LIFE you can begin again!